Haircuts

Teaching Tips

Blue Level 4

This book focuses on the phonemes **/ear/air/**.

Before Reading

- Discuss the title. Ask readers what they think the book will be about. Have them briefly explain why.
- Ask readers to sort the words on page 3. Read the sounds and words together.

Read the Book

- Encourage readers to break down unfamiliar words into units of sound. Then, ask them to string the sounds together to create the words.
- Urge readers to point out when the focused phonics phonemes appear in the text.

After Reading

- Encourage children to reread the book independently or with a friend.
- Ask readers to name other words with /ear/ or /air/ phonemes. On a separate sheet of paper, have them write the words out.

© 2024 Booklife Publishing
This edition is published by arrangement with Booklife Publishing.

North American adaptations © 2024 Jump!
5357 Penn Avenue South
Minneapolis, MN 55419
www.jumplibrary.com

Decodables by Jump! are published by Jump! Library.
All rights reserved. No part of this book may be reproduced in any form without written permission from the publisher.

Library of Congress Cataloging-in-Publication Data is available at www.loc.gov or upon request from the publisher.

ISBN: 979-8-88996-822-1 (hardcover)
ISBN: 979-8-88996-823-8 (paperback)
ISBN: 979-8-88996-824-5 (ebook)

Photo Credits

Images are courtesy of Shutterstock.com. With thanks to Getty Images, Thinkstock Photo and iStockphoto. Cover – Pair Srinrat. 4–5 – BearFotos, Pixel-Shot. 6–7 – Africa Studio, Maliutina Anna. 8–9 – Aksinia Prokhorova, SFROLOV. 10–11 – a35mmporhora, Alex Vog. 12–13 – NikolaJankovic, Roman Samborskyi. 14–15 – FXQuadro, LDarko. 16 – Shutterstock.

Can you sort all the words on this page into two groups?

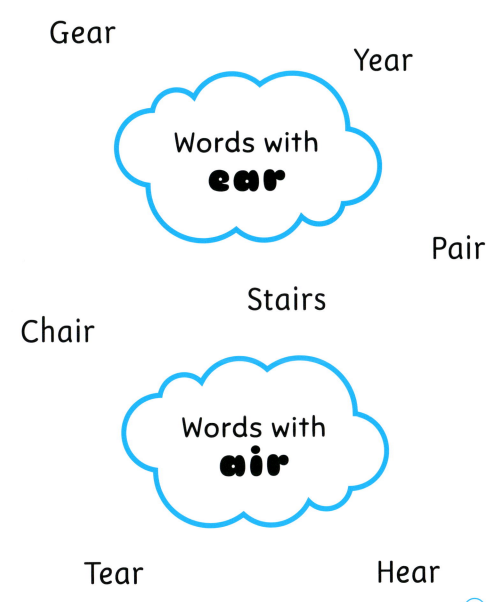

What happens when you get a haircut?

You sit in a chair to get a haircut. This chair is big and black.

Chair

A cape will catch the hair that is cut off.

Cape

Snip, snip. The hair is cut near the top.

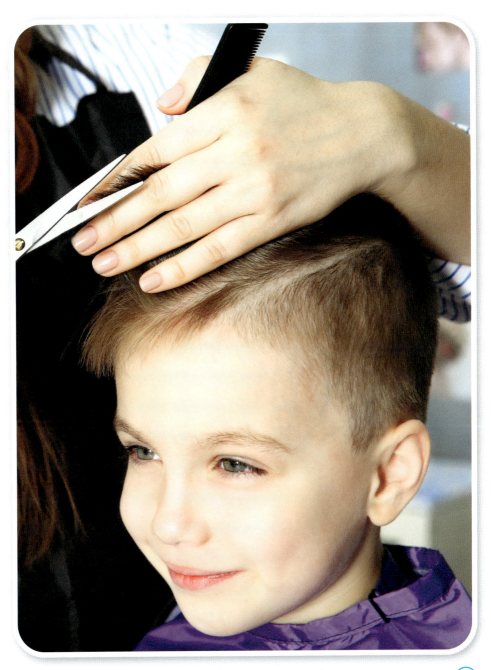

The clippers buzz near his ear. They trim the hair to the right length.

Clippers

Her hair is long. She needs a trim. She will get a little bit cut off near her back.

They might need to pin long hair up with a clip.

Clip

They gather up a lock of hair and cut it near the end.

Beards can be cut and trimmed.
The man will need to sit still.

They trim it near his neck and near his ear.

They trim some beard hair near his lip. It is neat now.

It can feel good to get a haircut.

Sound out each word. Does it have an /ear/ or /air/ sound?

gears

pair

fear

fair